T0100324

THE ANIMAL IS CHEMICAL

The Animal Is Chemical

POEMS

HADARA BAR-NADAV

FOUR WAY BOOKS
TRIBECA

LIBRARY OF CONGRESS CATALOGING-IN-PUBLICATION DATA

Names: Bar-Nadav, Hadara, author.

Title: The animal is chemical / by Hadara Bar-Nadav.

Description: New York : Four Way Books, 2024.

Identifiers: LCCN 2023031710 (print) | LCCN 2023031711 (ebook) | ISBN 9781961897007 (trade paperback) | ISBN 9781961897014 (ebook)

Subjects: LCGFT: Poetry.

Classification: LCC PS3602.A73 A83 2024 (print) | LCC PS3602.A73 (ebook) | DDC 811/.6--dc23/eng/20230717

LC record available at https://lccn.loc.gov/2023031710

LC ebook record available at https://lccn.loc.gov/2023031711

This book is manufactured in the United States of America and printed on acid-free paper.

Four Way Books is a not-for-profit literary press. We are grateful for the assistance we receive from individual donors, public arts agencies, and private foundations including the NEA, NEA Cares, Literary Arts Emergency Fund, and the New York State Council on the Arts, a state agency.

We are a proud member of the Community of Literary Magazines and Presses.

Funding for this book was provided in part by a generous donation in memory of John J. Wilson.

For my family, across the generations

What are you waiting for—
have faith in my chemical compassion.
　　　　　　—Wisława Szymborska, "Advertisement," Trans. Stanisław
　　　　　　Barańczak, from *Poems New and Selected*

we drink you mornings and noontime we drink you evenings
we drink and we drink
　　　　　　—Paul Celan, "Death Fugue," Trans. Pierre Joris, from *Memory*
　　　　　　Rose into Threshold Speech: The Collected Earlier Poetry

This pharmakon, *this "medicine," this philter, which acts as both remedy*
and poison, already introduces itself into the body of the discourse with all its
ambivalence. This charm, this spellbinding virtue, this power of fascination,
can be—alternately or simultaneously—beneficent or maleficent.
　　　　　　—Jacques Derrida, "Plato's Pharmacy," Trans. Barbara
　　　　　　Johnson, from *Dissemination*

CONTENTS

I.

Dybbuk

My horns are disappearing,
parts of my furred ears
rub away in the red wind.

Here, the wind can take you
in pieces—

> my long Semitic nose
> and curly hair like a calligraphy
> of barbed wire.

Someone is trying to burn the girl
out of me.

Diamonds line my eye sockets,
diamonds in my fever-lit brain.
My neck, a fat matchstick.

I am such spectacular light—shock
of incarnadine that ignites
even the shadows.

There are no shadows here, only
five golden finches rising

> like a hand into the blistering
> crown of a cherry tree.

A myth in which a god sets us
on fire and then sets us free.

The Singing Pills

I spit up the pills
that look like pills,

place them back inside
the orange safety bottle,

place the bottle next to
vitamins, aspirin, glue,

then hit the backspace key
and delete

       the scene now
       chroma white and starry.

Evening retreats
into day and the light

       does not yet hurt.

I smile all day long
and erase the trance of fire

each time it erupts
(delete, delete).

Each of my dead
holds a torch

inside me, bubbling
up my throat,

lungs gummed
with creosote.

I reverse into the early
morning blankery

when the pills still
sing me to sleep,

deep in the blue milk
of oblivion,

all of my wicks
for the moment unlit.

The laundry in piles
absent of bodies.

Each version of myself
is a day collapsed

in a flowered basket—

half fog, half sludge,
and twinkling.

My chemical sleep
ordered at the drugstore.

My pharmacist, my god,
my automatic refill,

        please, quell
        and quiet me.

I am an ordinary I
unfree from history.

Wolf Child

—Babi Yar, Kiev, September 1941

A girl rose
out of a wolf,

peeled the soft fur
back, ripped

      across her hips.

The animal consumed
from the inside.

What have I done
to survive—

      wrist bones
      still wrenched,

      electricity
      of breath

      wired
      through my teeth.

Feral, febrile,
fear-streaked.

The bloodline
severed here—.

I had been left
for dead in a forest

of emerald dreams,
scaling

the nightmare ravine—

      30 meters wide,
      150 meters long,

      15 meters deep
      and deep and deep.

The bodies: layer
upon sloppy layer

      like a botched
      jelly cake.

I ate what I needed,
my mouth flooded

      with ink—blueberries,
      blackberries, the sour

      crush of black
      currants—

and slept in a robe
of cold skin.

> *You can't catch me.*
> *You can't*
> > *catch me.*

The earth's jaw
opening.

Ventriloquist

The old wound is speaking
again through my back,

       carving its blood alphabet.

For days I can only crawl
from one side of pain

       to another, leashed
       to lightning—

       neon shooting
       through my jaw.

The pills and the pills,
white circular selves,

       the slippery self
       slipping, unselfing.

Remember to relax
my teeth (*Relax your teeth*).

Kundalini recoiling then
lashing forth, spring

       of metallic hisses.

My voice like a voyeur,
no, a ventriloquist

        fisting up my spine,
        forcing a moan.

My mouth cracks
open, unhinged, thrown

        by herniated suns
        teething on bone.

Queen of Collapse

Queen of disappearing, the girl in me gone

Queen of sweet milk, blisters, sweat

Queen as the night opens its mouth and cries

      The dreamthroat, blackthroat, barbaric guest

Queen seized by wide white jaws

My subjects all turn cannibal, animal, maul

Their love gigantic, their never-ending need

Queen claimed by the smallest fists

Queen of the body count, fingers, shadows, toes

Warped by war and sleeplessness, we are a thousand years old

Queen of the corpse I invite inside for a glass of rain

      The rain coming down like gravel over our heads

My mother's face ripples across my face, across my child's face

Queen of collapse, our hunger everlasting

The Ancestors Take the Reins of My Throat

There is always a we
        in my mouth, huddled

against my teeth. I start
        to speak and out pours

smoke with a leathered
        bit of tongue.

Numbles on a notebook
        spread out to dry.

Numbers inked onto
        the vellum skin of history.

This is a taxidermist's art,
        carve and scrape

down. Assemble grief,
        plaster, and paint,

a little paste
        for gold glass eyes.

Didn't the neighbor's cat
        stay obediently

frozen in an orange circle
        of light by the front door,

curled up there, forevered,
        a furred offering,

gutted, bent, leashed
        by love, as I am

a shell for others—
        my bit bitten, lips

peeled wide,
        the hollowed body

filled with cotton, wire,
        and the wind of ghosts.

Mindfield

No history here. No death. No siblings. Eleven who never disappeared in the Camps. I did not know them. They were never born. Eleven nameless question marks. My mother was from no city (Bratislava). My mother never lived (a tiny ghost lighting candles candles candles in Jerusalem). Father was a blur in a black suit stepping onto a train. He traded our family. Traitor. Two-timer. Time bomb. I have no family. I took a new name. Stories scorched behind me. What day is this? Am I born? Brand-new and naked like a baby, swaddled, clean. Above me, the blinding gold of a ruptured egg. The sun so swollen I can barely see.

Descend

Pain scales, scalds, radiates along
the crumbling spire of the self

A network of needles and nerves—
90,000 miles on fire

In one scale faces frown or weep,
in another words descend

Pain descends through your face

Point to the face that looks
like pain—your flat-lined mouth

X marks the spot on the outline
of a body—face rubbed out

78 words describe pain, every word
selected for you

> *searing, wrenching, wretched, shooting,*
> *cutting, suffocating, terrifying, vicious*

Point to your pain and a woman
writes it down

Say it clearly (with scalding hands)

I can feel each one of my nerve endings,
says your dead father

I can no longer hold up my own torso,
you say to the wall

Ragged lace of each breath
(your conversation crawls)

There are questions one must ask pain
(inside your OxyContin cloud)

Can you stand? Sit?
Have normal sexual relations?

Complete household tasks?

How long is each day, how long
each lashing hour?

How red your pain, how blue?

Your pain goal on a scale of one
centimeter to oblivion?

Earn a score of one for no crying,
higher scores for

grimace, groaning, moaning,
screaming (high-pitched/not)

Map the distance between

drilling and *stabbing,*
gnawing and *crushing,*
punishing and *killing*

Measure it in breaths
(whir, whir, whir, whir)

Finally, no words contain you   .

I Took the Drugs

marked sleep for sleep and the drugs marked joy to trudge through grief and the yellow drugs to crack my Vaseline smile, ooze trickling the length of my spine, the hair on my arms electrically charged. The stop-my-mind-from-shaking drugs for blood-dipped dreams, the stop-crying drugs that left me hazed in a hangover for empty weeks, the taste of copper licking my lips. I took the drugs for side effects, the drugs for drugs, bottle-shape they shoved me in, body of sludge. Call me the great undead with a pharmaceutical edge and a head full of mud. But I believe, if I believe hard enough, if I am a believer on my knees, praying for ease, oblivion, please. The pink circle by day, blue ovoid by night, white pearl for when my chest ruptures into flame. Lullabied by the dead and the history of the dead. My wounds flickering beneath my skin.

Death by Design

In my dream I am
        a pile of chalk,
        a pile of death.

I want to walk
        to the skin closet
        and pick out another coat,

but I have no hands,
        no wool, no feet. Fire
        has nearly erased me.

Ovens by Topf and Sons,
        high capacity designs
        for death—

        double muffle,
        triple muffle,

        eight-muffle progression
        of incineration—

        that wed our skin
        to brick and wind and dirt.

Some part of us refused
        the purest expression
        of perfect erasure.

Stubborn bone, ash
        that sticks to the backs
        of throats. I love you,

I choke you,
        who forevered me,
        fed me to the light.

I dream I light
        your bed on fire
        with a bit of finger bone.

I am electrical,
        volatile, my yellow
        cry whistling through

your chest, blistering
        you from the inside.
        In your dreams,

we crush your mouth
        with the blackened dust
        of our million names,

and like a chorus
        of blue flames
        lick you nightly.

II.

[Your mind is night]

—from the Tretinoin Gel (Retin A) package insert

Your

       mind

       is

       night.

Your

eyes   open wounds.

Your whole face

       may

             become

                  skeletal.

       FIRE

       is

       your

       nature.

       FLAME

       is

       your

       friend.

Deep inside your skin
New Zealand White rabbits
        report

excessively troublesome
       feeling[s] of warmth,
       inflammatory lesions,
       peeling
       of the total body surface,

      a red   blistered
                     day.

Question   your
                     toxic
      nature.

Question
      the   human
           risk.

Death
is excreted in human milk
       with
       alcohol, spices,
and   lime.

You can't wash it away.

Use   extreme
caution.

        YOU
        ARE FLAMMABLE.

[Infect this page]

—from the Ceftriaxone (Rocephin) drug information from Medline Plus

Infect
this page.

Inject
the
blood
of
work.

Kill
your   need to
question
this

garbage   art,

a written list of all
problems of the heart.

Someone who is sick
is
at
war,

                                    the victim of
                                    your normal
                                    American
                                    diet
                                    of
                                    disease
                    and pain.

Take   an
ax
to your
tongue.

You should begin to feel better
                        or get worse.

O cloudy
day.

O bloody   month.

[I should know emergency]

—from the Sertraline Hydrochloride (Zoloft) package insert

I should know

               emergency.

Call your   new

               feelings.

Follow up   with your

           depression,

           dangerous impulses,

           or dying.

Unusually grand ideas
risk
trouble.

Excessive happiness

               should

               stop.

Your

          disorder

          disorder

          disorder

                    disorder
                    disorder
                    disorder

                    and feelings of failure
                    may
                    not go away.

For active   sexual problems,
shaking   and
loss of consciousness

call   pharmaceuticals.

[Trust us]

—from the Cyclobenzaprine (Flexeril) patient and prescribing information and MedlinePlus

Trust
us.

                Relax.
           Relax.
     Relax.

Relax   the brain and nervous system,
the mouth.

Swallow
     your
     heart.

       Swallow   it
       with applesauce.

          Swallow without chewing.

Your
heart   has
a history of
     failure.

Your
heart
is a
blue   gelatin
sphere

consume[d]
          by   red
                                        thoughts.

                                        Admit
                  hearing voices that do not exist.

Carry
them   with you.

                              Pain
          comes
          to
                              crush
          and   eat you.

          Ask
          your doctor and pharmacist

to keep
you   safe,

stroke
your face
                     with
                     tenderness
          like
                     a child.

[You are awake]

—from the Tobradex (Tobramycin and Dexamethasone) package information (US and UK)

You are awake
for
48 hours

or 24 days.

Shake.

Twist off
your head

in front of a mirror if it helps.

Do not touch.

Do not
   talk.

Do not
   drive.

Do not
   sweat.

Do not
   screw.

Do not worry.

Do not take
       drugs.

Do not use the bottle.

Do not
       breath[e].

       Manifestations of
       white
       harm.

Mother
please
       help
       me
       be
purified
as   water.

Gently release
       me   one drop at a time.

[Before difficulty]

—from the Albuterol patient information from MedlinePlus and Proair
patient information

Before

difficulty.

Before

chronic.

Before

four times a day.

Before

but will not cure your condition.

Step 1
Step 3
Step 7

Breathe.

Figure B
Figure I
Figure K

Breathe.

Do not stop

breathing.

Remember
this
last

        paradoxical
        disclaimer.

        You are
    no longer
  plastic.

You are
    pounding
    in your throat.

Your lungs
    are foreign objects,
      wrong   and   wrong.

Count down
how many
      seconds
      you have left.

Air
will change to red
       and shake.

Breath
       no longer
       a part of the body.

III.

Biopsy in Pink

I arrive on a metal table, my underlife
flooding the screen. I am famous—the entire

picture, edge to edge, unseemly bloom,
a van Dongen with too much rouge.

Take a piece from the blackened whole
and spread me under a microscope.

I'll be the one wearing flowers, a hand-sized
hibiscus rippling behind my ear like

a warning with sequins and foghorn:
abnormal cell cluster at 9 and 4.

A clock in my breast and the seconds
twitch, inching forward like scalpels.

My scintillating cilia full of frill, thrill
of the grotesque, its misshapen promise.

The doctor says, *Pick a shape for your scar:*
a frown or grin, incised across my heart.

Now smile for the giant eye of God.

Loop (in Dirt and Gold)

I sold the necklace, my name written in gold.
I wanted a baby. The doctors fed me lies,
Clomid, and unicorns. I sold the necklace
my father gifted me, a gold memento,
its blood-filled cost. I was finished with him,
ten years dead. I wanted a baby. The doctors
bled me—needle needle needle—until
I was more wound than skin. Pincushion blue,
skeleton ache, zombie of want for the child
who would not wake. I was a child for my father
who left me again and again, who wanted and then
did not. I failed the gods, their nullifying tests,
and wanted to be dead like the child I lost,
buried deep in the earth, a crumb of gold.

The Selection (Intrauterine Insemination)

So many of you and not
nearly enough.

Five large eggs, their empty
promises.

      A legion of nevers.

I plunged each needle
in, I plunged inside

      a pinch of fat.

Bring on the supernumerary.

The nurse's dull speech
about "selection"

      lined in electric wire.

Here I hunt the perfect
egg, miracle of eugenics—

      its bright blond smile.

Select out, select in,
pick off the blotched

or misshapen, small
afterthoughts legible

only in the ledger
of delible facts.

Graph and pulse
cancelled—

       a line run through like a sudden
       blade.

Would I have a child,
a chance, or five,

and would they all perish.

Bottom Feeder

Lost to my own loss, inside
its tidal weight and pull.

The almost-child, the not-
quite formed.

Seahorse in a blood sea,
her tail hooked to my core.

A girl with a heart who died
inside me, a girl who was almost

breath, spine, curl, whole,

who was and is and will be
chasm—

        so I am coffin, hull.

I died inside me, scraped clean.
Loss moved in and sank me.

A Coffin of Clouds

The dead make a kite
the size of god—

      omni-present,
      omni-eyed.

Four kinds of god: feather,
blanket, cotton, sheet.

The clouds offer
their sums, their minuses.

Our vast wreckage—

      ghost opal,
      blighted egg,

      a blood sea.

Entire eyefulls
of endings.

Weren't we at last
provisional,

      delusional, more shell
      than whole.

My lack of compass,
composure.

I throw out
a shallow noun,

      anemic invectives.

Fuck you, sky,
you liar,

where a god has gone
to die.

      Firelit. Ghostlit.
      Smothered in reds.

No one survives
heaven.

Black Screen (Kidney Ultrasound)

*Nazi guards screened individuals for their potential to work upon entering
concentration camps. Those sent to the left were killed; those sent to the right
were assigned forced labor. Through the Aktion T4 Program, Nazi medical staff
euthanized 300,000 people, including children, with mental and physical disabilities.*

One small, smaller
       as if shy, shrinking
       in the red unlit world.

Trifling to her twin.
       Minikin. Scrap
       of unfit flesh.

Hanger-on, damaged
       like Aunt Teresa
       called *deaf-n-dumb*

during the war,
       with no words
       to rename herself,

who stepped off
       a train and vanished
       to the left,

to the left,
       whose body I carry
       inside my own.

Faulty girl,

      incurable, unworthy,

      disavowed.

You should have that

      looked at, my doctor says,

      and I can't stop.

Every Object Is Someone

My father, my blue cup. The cherry table in the kitchen, my father again. The red lamp overhead bobbing like a half moon, my toothless grandmother. See her inside the picture viewer, a green plastic tube the size of my thumb. She sits on a shelf with hair pins and an ivory lace pillowcase sewn by her sister, whose face I wear. Her eyes and lips. Olga who hanged herself after Kristallnacht. Night of breaking, breaking. Every object alive and not alive. Every object a little glitter inside. A glow that could burn this house down.

Harvest

      Silence didn't exist
until the 14th century.

      Until the 14th century
there was only noise, or silence
itself was silenced, unmapped
in language—a hollow
of silence waiting to rise.

      When my mother tells me
to break her jaw after she dies—
the titanium plate inside
worth a mint—I have only silence.
Why let the crematorium keep
the precious metal after melting
her down to four pounds of ash?

      Does she really envision me
with a hacksaw and power drill,
suddenly dentist and demented,
harvesting her for parts then
dropping off her faceless remains
for a hot, prepaid date with a furnace?

      How horrible a daughter I am.
How loving. How Judaism forbids
us to cremate or deface the body,
though mother longs to be god
of her own death.

Is she thinking of Nazis,
their payload of Jewish gold
chiseled from the teeth of
a million nameless bones?
What is disturbing a corpse when
the corpse is your mother
asking you to hack her apart?

Her mouth hanging open.
My mouth hanging open.
Her mouth is my mouth.

Silence rises, rushes out
like a bonfire blistering the space
between us. The sound of a mouth
that can no longer speak.

Death Party

My mother assigns
the couches names—

> *Garbage, Salvation*
> *Army,* *T* (my favored sibling)—

she wants to control
what remains.

Clouds strain through
threadbare seams.

The legs have gnawed
off their own skin,

trembling atop
the crippled feet of lions.

The crematorium
has been paid in full.

The mausoleum
accepts installments.

The final plans
are final

until she changes
her mind again.

Her mind changes.

I am not invited to attend
to such matters with a pen

and Post-its in hand,
to walk her final rooms

perfumed with Mademoiselle
and moth balls.

Death is an activity,
a dream, a pursuit,

as her yellow notes
float to the ground—

       a ticker-tape parade
       of miniature ghosts.

What is fixed then
flies away.

The furniture, the family,
the finally gone.

Laughter rises
from her cracked teacup.

The House Is a Difficult Text

Line breaks
trace the windows.

      Blankness follows.

      More moments
      of blank.

Show them
what burned:

              every   thing.

The house, her red hair,
the roots.

This is the difficult
next—

      who fell asleep
      on the flower-printed couch,

      whose cigarette wore
      a bright coral ring?

      Her lips, her slow
      breath, her dream.

Newspapers mounded
around her,

a paper maze
three-feet high,

       and her body
       at the hot center,

       her body as kindling,
       tinderboxed.

She died inside
a dying house

returning itself
to dust.

The difficult part
is two deaths:

a palpable
emptiness,

       a field.

IV.

[Carry an identification card]

—from the Dexamethasone drug information from Medline Plus

Carry an identification card that indicates

      your body,   your land,
      certain forms of   blood.

COVID,
cancer, colitis,
      confusion.

          Large doses
     of loss.

If you

         miss
         miss
    miss   your
             mind,

if you

    need to
         protect
    the lace
    of your
    heart,

if the   victim has collapsed,
               send a report to the   Administration
               of combat.

                             Write down
                             signs of
                             trouble,

the matter you cough up,
                        tartrazine,
                        gray or green,
                        redness

      bruising
      your throat.

      I   will
      hear
              you
you   you
      you.

Tell
        me
your
history of
war.

[Life eats breath]

*—from the Midazolam (Versed) patient information from Medline Plus
and Kaiser Permanente*

Life
eat[s]
breath.

Death
eat[s]
pain.

How helpful is this
verse   to you?

The author
will watch you closely
at   night

with the help of a machine
and
a nurse.

This
injection comes as a solution to
prevent any memory of the event.

Call the poison
poison.

                    Terror
                    will prepare and measure your dose.

Keep a written list of
verse
to carry with you in case of emergencies.

You
may
not
get
        well.

You
may
not
go
        home.

[The animal is chemical]

—from the Fenbendazole (Panacur) product label

The animal   is
chemical,
CARNIVOROUS,
sick.

For your
      safety
keep   families
in
a controlled room
for 60   days in a row.

Contain the
worms.

Hook,
whip, tape.

Children
must be fully consumed
during the hunting season.

Grizzly
offering of the main meal.

Believe   the parasite.

The animal

                          remains.

[I am altered, terminal, skeletal]

—from the Fentanyl package insert and Medline Plus drug information

I am

                altered,

       terminal,

                skeletal.

The hours

                blunt

                me,

                dine

                on

                my

head.

                Sign a form

acknowledging you understand the risks

                that

                erase you.

                Euphoria

is released slowly into the blood,

severe and unpredictable,

paralyzing
my
open heart.

Death
is
patient,

monitoring
the muscles of respiration,
neck,   eye,
and eyelash.

The brain

is
shivering
in human milk.

The brain

says

manufacture
light.

Dreams
decrease the
urge to breathe
and   end with wire cutters

          tearing along the perforations,
          pink side facing up.

    You may
    feel dizzy, sleepy,
    minty,
    a gentle bubbling feeling,

    until   you
    completely
    dissolve.

[Come, it is almost time]

*—from the Ondansetron (Zofran) package information from Medline Plus
and Prescriber's Digital Reference*

Come,

        it is almost time

                to end.

Nausea, vomiting,
chemotherapy, radiotherapy.

This treatment   is
        a killer.

Eyes, lips, tongue, throat, hands, feet, ankles, legs
rapidly disintegrating.

        Your
        blue
        ache.

There is little information
        shown on the label
        of
        your
        yellow   face,
                forgotten
                and plain.

You
are   not
special
and

last

for a short time.

An hour
live[d]

gently
on
this page.

V.

Prayer (with Percocet)

Lost in a cemetery again, a maze
       of losses: section C, row 6, plot 18

Red roses, rows of endings,
       and the scent of oranges

At the center, I am surrounded by stone,
       leave a pebble behind

Didn't I hope a pill would keep
       my father's heart alive forever?

Didn't I hope a pill would take
       care of it?

The gods of science were wrong—ghosts
       floating off in their white coats

What can you do for me, ghost-
       colored pill asleep in my pocket?

Miniature moon who could crush me,
       who is almost good

In the morning, I check the label
       and see my own face in flames

One pill and I can watch my pain
       from across the room

I slowly slide my breath between
the knives in my neck

My sunrise of painkillers
blood-orange

Ligature

The surgery was open heart.

I was cut this way. Whipsawed.

Continent divided. From this, a spectacular wound.

Sealed shut, but for my awe-filled mouth,

monitored, machined, dabbed with Vaseline.

I wasn't there. I was on the moon

floating in a chemical pool of fentanyl—

heavy cloud of black oil rimmed in gold.

Awake, and frozen. Awake, eyes open then

crashing back into the dumb moon skull.

Metal taste like a rusty length of pipe.

Every breath ever-after wed to its scar—

frosting-thick ripple of pink. Pig-colored.

I am forbidden to put my teeth on it (and I do).

Wound where the light grows

        growls

        unheals

and remembers what is written there.

Pharmakon

I can erase pain with the golden touch of one hand, light vibrating in waves

and erase my mother's collapsing knees and her hippocampus where her
      family screams from the bottom of a mass grave

and the right side of my face where my mother cries in my sleep and
      a migraine rakes my eye socket

and the bottom half of my rickety spine, so my torso and waist fog and float—
      iridescent liquid smoke (my glittering unraveling)

and my father's oversized heart that twitches in my hands for whole minutes
      before it melts into an ice-colored dove and vanishes

I erase a year with a drunken wraith who could not keep an erection (though
      I pocket his violet eyes as souvenirs)

and my son crying for milk, goodbye voice box and sky-scraping tantrums

and my ears, skin-cups plucked from either side of my skull

gone pill, poison, the scapegoat's coughed-up song (every grief-blown
      note of it)

gone bedroom I once shared with myself and the mattress where death spilled
      out, a child-sized cloud leaking from my lips

who could live with me now, ghost of a ghost without form or name?

Mute

Why can I not speak in dreams?

      Uncle Mangler, Murderer, Mengele
      playing with twins in his zoo again,

stitching together the skins
of their gypsy backs.

      Whole barrels of cream-
      colored legs and the children's

heads preserved and shipped
to universities in Graz and Berlin.

      Specimens for the advancement
      of silence.

Don't forget the still living
eyes injected with dye.

      How to make both blue,
      correct heterochromia, root out

the brown, brute Jew.

      The dissection done, a shower
      with Zyklon B or 14 shots

of chloroform into twin hearts
(two by two by *hush*).

      My doctor of dreams, Angel
      of Death who sutures

closed my *useless mouth*.
I am mute and dumb

      and would call you Uncle
      if I could find my tongue.

Pleas[e]

—From statements made by Nazi doctors and medical personnel during the 1947 Nuremberg Trials for their war crimes and medical experiments on Jews, Roma, political prisoners, and others.

I was competent responsible   surgical.

I   was

this pile of rubble.

*

I feel   free of

humanity.

*

I repeat

I never had feeling.

Human beings
deserve death.

*

My actions   were clean.

*

Craving my   beloved Father

*

I devoted myself to

true belief.

Good
filled me.

*

I never sinned.

*

I never worked

for medical science.

*

Typhus and malaria
serve the good of humanity.

*

Euthanasia
of mankind   was

*

never directed by any sentiment.

*

Transgressions and
experiments on human beings   seemed
peaceful.

*

I could
administer   difficult
                             care.

Did I.

*

Father
        I am proud
        blood with unceasing fervor.

*

The motive   is devotion.

*

I have acted as a soldier, and as a soldier
                I do not
                complain.

*

My children

will believe that their father

[i]s an enemy.

*

The spiteful

twist of

thorn bushes

will be the appropriate answer.

*

I have seen how

I have nothing.

*

Console me.

*

Thank me.

*

Please,

*

I never failed

my Father.

Dirty

Dirty dirty Jew. Dirty dirty dirty. Jew money. Jew thief. Jew miser. Jew greed. Jew *Arbeit Macht Frei*. Jew sweat. Jew grease. Jew hair: kinky, oily, dirty black. Jew nose: lip-low, an oversized hook. *Hath not Jew eyes?* Almond-shaped, shit-brown or wet ash. Jew lightning. Jew star. Jew flame. Jew teeth: a whole harvest of gold. Jew skeleton. Jew soap. Jew mutilation, hypothermia, and sterilization by X-ray. Jew breeder of infectious disease—malaria, tuberculosis, typhus. Jew showers. Jew clouds of carbon monoxide and Zyklon B. Jew history: fake. Jew lies: erased. Tattooed degenerates. Jew rats hidden in attics, stuffed under floorboards, into ovens, trains. Jew millions. Masses. Mud. Graves. Jew extinction in a Jew museum. Terezin: a Jew country club, a red sea crossed by the Red Cross. Jew music, operas, plays. Jew humor. Jew brain. That toothless laugh, such howling.

The Hook of History

Under the guise of alcohol I grow charming and unrecognizable.
One numbness is not as good as another. My heart diluted with ice.

The past arrives with its staple gun and rusted alphabet.
Flinch and fill in the watery blanks.

Nazis chase my grandmother until she dies. Nazis chase my mother in her sleep.
In her sleep, her mother cries through her mouth.

The Museum of Nostalgia. The Museum for the Extinction of Nostalgia.
The Museum of Natural History.

Newspapers mindlessly blow around the ruins of Mike's Café.
Starlings hunt for crumbs among cobblestones.

The walls of the Shalom Hotel blink from pink to paper white.
Ghosts of women sing in the stairwells through mottled lips.

In the morning, suffering circles itself and repeats.
Children in the courtyard scream and scream, and there is joy in this.

Dear Father (with Fever)

To you I have nothing
to say, you who are not here.

Feverish on this gray couch
in a gray year in a gray world.

The viral load of Earth multiplying,
the viral load of melancholia.

Big droplets and small, aerosols.
The children harbor, fester, super
spreaders, and yet, their sweet milk scent.

I see your face in my children's faces
and cannot escape the loss of you

cycling, repeating each morning,
mourning, morning like a giant
bell in my brain.

Grief in the time of plague.
Love in the time of same.

You are a giant bell that beats
my brain each morning,
mourning, morning.

I cannot escape your face that ghosts
my children's faces.

Their sweet, milk-scented heads
harbor and fester. Super
spreaders, big and small.

Melancholia multiplies like a viral load
in this gray world

in this gray year on a gray couch
where I fever and cough fear.

You are not here, I say to you nothing
you can hear.

The Parenthesis

opens its hook mouth, hook smile

Wide and toothless like a baby in pure howl

Like the whole world could fall inside

Groping for underlanguage, underwords in a muted register

Words underneath, inside, closer to the dust at the back of the throat

Before death, after the breathing tube

Gurgling, guttering

Can you make sense of this?

The wide hook will never close its terrible mouth

Metallic lick of loss, each hard swallow

All language is a whisper reborn, breathscraped, bloodscraped, air hunger

Before death came we smiled

The heart beating until there is *nothing you can feel with your hand*

Touch and its blank-eyed stare

The ground heaving, lifting up

        and the blank after

Sail

I used to live inside my father
now I live inside the fragile air

My head shifts too quickly quakes
against its thinking about shadows

My hand appears three times in various grisaille
(meaning pale blue sails and my shit-poor French)

When my father died my body fell
inside me, a crush of concrete

                    days of dust and buckling,
                    gravel-burned knees

And then came a turn, an inverse

                    pure paranoid balloon

I was flying up unmoored, unhooked
abandoned by gravity

                    flying up in my ice dress, ice skin

Breath of a corpse death sliding between
blood and flesh and flesh and wind

(nothing held me here)

Ice moon, a cheap dime in the sky

I touched its shiny fear

Cloud

Vapor, cell, wish,

       spot on the lung
       roiling.

Ash cloud, dust cloud,
lilac smoke.

Shape of ache,
granular disappearance.

Small weight of crushed
bone.

The Brilliant Fragments

To kneel by the cochineal
head of the dead.

Fragments—grammar
broken along the way.

The birds drop
at my feet,

      eleven of them, sucked
      out of the sky, whole.

I return home.
I report the details.

The men who attempt
to control animals

tell me to bag each one,
though I am afraid

to touch their bright
stillness—

      the blank eyes
      in their blank heads.

      It is all wrong

as are the chemical clouds
drifting from the fields

where the cows make
us milk and meat.

The sunsets beautifully hued:

      oozy pink,
        infected apricot.

Day after day
of wrong color.

Then farm trucks encircle
the town and spray

a silver-white fog
to *neutralize* the air.

Twinkling stitched
to the sky

      like ghosts
        beading the wind.

NOTES

"Dybbuk" is inspired by Jewish folklore that depicts the dybbuk as a disembodied spirit, which possesses a human host. Women with mental health conditions were often said to be possessed by dybbuks.

"Wolf Child" refers to the massacre on September 29-30, 1941, when approximately 33,771 Jews were murdered by the Nazis at Babi Yar, a ravine in Kiev. This massacre was among the largest single mass murders of Jews during World War II. This poem is also indebted to my friend's grandmother who shared her story of surviving the Holocaust. As a child, she was shot in the shoulder and chest, then pretended to be dead while lying in a mass grave before fleeing and saving herself. This poem's opening image was inspired by Kiki Smith's sculpture *Rapture* and her wolf series.

"Mindfield" is in memory of my grandmother Bella Rosen (1908-1990) and eleven of her siblings who were murdered in the Holocaust.

"Death by Design" refers to Topf and Sons, the company that designed incineration ovens for Nazi concentration camps. Topf and Sons claimed that their ovens provided "the purest expression of perfection in cremation technology."

"Loop (in Dirt and Gold)" is for baby V. (2012-2012).

"Black Screen (Kidney Ultrasound)" is in memory of my Great Aunt Teresa Herrmannova (dates unknown), who was murdered in the Holocaust. This poem refers to the common practice of Nazi guards screening individuals for their potential to work upon entering concentration camps. Those sent to the left were immediately killed; those sent to the right were assigned forced labor. Through the Aktion T4 Program, Adolf Hitler directed Nazi medical staff to involuntarily euthanize some 300,000 people, including infants and children, who had mental and physical disabilities. These murdered individuals were referred to as "life unworthy of life."

"Every Object Is Someone" is for my father Moty Bar-Nadav (1940-2007), my grandmother Hedva/Hattie Lowey (1903-1991), and my Great Aunt Olga Schnablova (1907-1933).

"The House Is a Difficult Text" is for my grandmother-in-law Jenny Clyde Satterfield (1915-1985).

"Mute" is based on medical experiments conducted by Josef Mengele, the lead physician of the medical research program at Auschwitz during World War II. Mengele experimented on over 3,000 children and was particularly interested in "treating" twins and individuals with spinal issues. Though he was referred to as the Angel of Death, he curiously asked the children he experimented on to call him Uncle. The experiments in the poem are actual experiments he performed on children, such as injecting ink into brown eyes to make them blue, performing amputations, and deliberately infecting children with diseases. He would then murder those he experimented on and mail their heads for further study to doctors and scientists working in universities throughout Germany—all in the name of science. Mengele was never punished for his crimes, but was hidden and protected by friends and family until his death.

"Pleas[e]" is an erasure based on final statements made by twenty-three Nazi doctors and medical personnel during the Nuremberg Trials for their war crimes and experiments on hundreds of thousands of people, including Jews, Romani, political prisoners, and others. I am indebted to Vivien Spitz's *Doctors from Hell: The Horrific Account of Nazi Experiments on Humans* (2005), which includes transcripts from this trial (Military Tribunal I, July 19, 1947).

"Dirty" quotes the phrase "Arbeit Macht Frei" ("work sets you free"), which was written across the entrance gate at Auschwitz. "Hath not Jew eyes" is adapted from Shylock in Shakespeare's play *The Merchant of Venice*. Terezin was a concentration camp in Czechoslovakia visited by the Red Cross. The Nazis enlisted the healthiest prisoners to, in effect, stage a play of a happy ghetto in order to fool the Red Cross into believing that Terezin was a place where individuals and families could thrive. The facts prove otherwise. Approximately 33,000 people died in Terezin. Another 88,000 people were deported from Terezin and sent to various death camps. Of the approximately 15,000 children sent to Terezin, fewer than 150 survived. (http://www.terezin.org/the-history-of-terezin/)

The pharmaceutical erasures are based on package inserts from medications my family has recently consumed. Package inserts contain life-saving information but are coded in medical jargon. Through the erasure form, I rewrite package inserts and create poems—human language in a human tongue. I literally dismantle package inserts by crossing out and rearranging the remaining text, and metaphorically dismantle power structures associated with the pharmaceutical industry. I hope these poems inform and empower people and perhaps even disarm the pharmaceutical industry, which is invested in selling us drugs that may or may not heal us.

*

I am immensely grateful to Jericho Brown, visionary poet, for believing in this book and awarding it the Levis Prize in Poetry. My sincere thanks to Martha Rhodes, Ryan Murphy, and the generous staff of Four Way Books for bringing this book into the world. Infinite gratitude to Rebecca Morgan Frank, Simone Muench, Kevin Prufer, and Allison Benis White, beloved friends who offered essential feedback and support during the writing of this book. Many thanks also to Cyrus Console, Erin Adair Hodges, Jenny Molberg, and Molly Peacock, whose insights helped me shape several of these poems, and to Bridget Lowe and Jameelah Lang for creative sustenance and friendship. To my sister Talie—thank you for your ongoing dedication to researching and recording our family history and for helping to find and name those we have lost. Your work is a blessing and a light. Boundless gratitude to my family, to my two children and my love, Scott Beattie, endlessly and always.

*

This book is in memory of approximately fifty of my family members who were murdered in the Holocaust, some of whose names appear below.
הכרבל ונורכיז

Hedvika Abeles (1870-1942)

Josef Abeles (1869-1942)

Jindrich Hajek (1882-1941)

Elvira (Ella) Frankenbusch (1903-unknown)

Frantizek Frankenbusch (1905-unknown)

Hermina Frankenbusch (1881-1944)

Josef Frankenbusch (1875-1944)

Buchbinder Frontisek (1905-unknown)

Evzenie Ganz (1888-1942)

Alfred Grunfeld (1876-1942)

Arnostka (Ernestine) Grunfeld (1869-1943)

Clara Grunfeld (1904-1944)

Marketa Grunfeld (1892-unknown)

Karla Goldschmid (unknown)

Karolina Goldschmid (1868-1943)

Josef Herrmannova (unknown)

Malvina Herrmannova (1880-1940)

Teresa Herrmannova (unknown)

Anna Krausova (Kraus) (1880-1942)

Klara Lindt (1904-1944)

Emilie (Emma) Lowy (1887-1942)

Franziska Lowy (Edelstein) (1855-1942)

Ida Lowy (1892-1943)

Otto Lowy (1887-1943)

Frantizek Minarik (1899-unknown)

Siblings of Bella Rosen:

Sibling #1 (unknown)

Sibling #2 (unknown)

Sibling #3 (unknown)

Sibling #4 (unknown)

Sibling #5 (unknown)

Sibling #6 (unknown)

Sibling #7 (unknown)

Sibling #8 (unknown)

Sibling #9 (unknown)

Sibling #10 (unknown)

Sibling #11 (unknown)

Jan Roudnicky (unknown)

Bohumil Schnabl (1866-1942)

Josef Schnabl (1904-1942)

Hans Schwarz (1897-1944)

Anna Silberstern (1850-1942)

Jan Simanek (1900-unknown)

Milada Stein (unknown)

Otto Stein (unknown)

Karel Stransky (unknown)

Rudolf Stransky (unknown)

Ida Truneckova (1892-1943)

Emma Zentner (1886-1942)

Gertruda Zentner (1910-1942)

Greta Zentner (1912-1943)

Further traces of all the above are missing.

    —From a letter to my grandfather, Joseph Lowey,
       November 1, 1946, from the Council of Jewish Communities

ACKNOWLEDGMENTS

Grateful acknowledgment is made to the editors of the following publications in which these poems or versions of these poems first appeared:

The Account

Action, Spectacle

American Literary Review

American Poetry Review

Barrow Street

The Believer

Colorado Review

Crazyhorse

Diode

The Florida Review

Green Mountains Review

The Kenyon Review

The Kenyon Review Online

Laurel Review

Los Angeles Review

Memorious

Mississippi Review

Poetry

Poets.org

Sprung Formal

Tin House

Tupelo Quarterly

Verse Daily

Thank you to the National Endowment for the Arts for a Fellowship in Poetry, which provided essential support during the writing of this manuscript. Thank you to *The Florida Review* for awarding several of these poems The Meek Award.

ABOUT THE AUTHOR

Hadara Bar-Nadav is the recipient of a National Endowment for the Arts Fellowship in Poetry, the Lucille Medwick Award from the Poetry Society of America, and other honors. Her award-winning books include *The New Nudity* (Saturnalia Books, 2017); *Lullaby (with Exit Sign)* (Saturnalia Books, 2013), awarded the Saturnalia Books Poetry Prize; *The Frame Called Ruin* (New Issues, 2012), Editor's Selection/Runner-Up for the Green Rose Prize; and *A Glass of Milk to Kiss Goodnight* (*Margie*/Intuit House, 2007), awarded the Margie Book Prize. She is also the author of two chapbooks, *Fountain and Furnace* (Tupelo Press, 2015), awarded the Sunken Garden Poetry Prize, and *Show Me Yours (Laurel Review*/Green Tower Press, 2010), awarded the Midwest Poets Series Prize. In addition, she is co-author with Michelle Boisseau of the best-selling textbook *Writing Poems, 8th ed.* (Pearson, 2011). Her poetry has appeared in *The American Poetry Review, The Believer, The Kenyon Review, The New Republic, Ploughshares, Poetry, Tin House*, and elsewhere. She is a Professor of English and teaches in the MFA program at the University of Missouri-Kansas City.

PUBLICATION OF THIS BOOK WAS MADE POSSIBLE
BY GRANTS AND DONATIONS. WE ARE ALSO GRATEFUL
TO THOSE INDIVIDUALS WHO PARTICIPATED IN
OUR BUILD A BOOK PROGRAM. THEY ARE:

Anonymous (14), Robert Abrams, Michael Ansara, Kathy Aponick, Jean Ball, Sally Ball, Clayre Benzadon, Adrian Blevins, Laurel Blossom, Adam Bohannon, Betsy Bonner, Patricia Bottomley, Lee Briccetti, Joel Brouwer, Susan Buttenwieser, Anthony Cappo, Paul and Brandy Carlson, Dan Clarke, Mark Conway, Elinor Cramer, Kwame Dawes, Michael Anna de Armas, John Del Peschio, Brian Komei Dempster, Rosalynde Vas Dias, Patrick Donnelly, Lynn Emanuel, Blas Falconer, Jennifer Franklin, John Gallaher, Reginald Gibbons, Rebecca Kaiser Gibson, Dorothy Tapper Goldman, Julia Guez, Naomi Guttman and Jonathan Mead, Forrest Hamer, Luke Hankins, Yona Harvey, KT Herr, Karen Hildebrand, Carlie Hoffman, Glenna Horton, Thomas and Autumn Howard, Catherine Hoyser, Elizabeth Jackson, Linda Susan Jackson, Jessica Jacobs and Nickole Brown, Lee Jenkins, Elizabeth Kanell, Nancy Kassell, Maeve Kinkead, Victoria Korth, Brett Lauer and Gretchen Scott, Howard Levy, Owen Lewis and Susan Ennis, Margaree Little, Sara London and Dean Albarelli, Tariq Luthun, Myra Malkin, Louise Mathias, Victoria McCoy, Lupe Mendez, Michael and Nancy Murphy, Kimberly Nunes, Susan Okie and Walter Weiss, Cathy McArthur Palermo, Veronica Patterson, Jill Pearlman, Marcia and Chris Pelletiere, Sam Perkins, Susan Peters and Morgan Driscoll, Maya Pindyck, Megan Pinto, Kevin Prufer, Martha Rhodes and Jean Brunel, Paula Rhodes, Louise Riemer, Peter and Jill Schireson, Rob Schlegel, Yoana Setzer, Soraya Shalforoosh, Mary Slechta, Diane Souvaine, Barbara Spark, Catherine Stearns, Jacob Strautmann, Yerra Sugarman, Arthur Sze and Carol Moldaw, Marjorie and Lew Tesser, Dorothy Thomas, Rushi Vyas, Martha Webster and Robert Fuentes, Rachel Weintraub and Allston James, Abby Wender and Rohan Weerasinghe, and Monica Youn.